Brighter Grammar

An English Grammar with Exercises

BOOK FOUR
New Edition

Phebean Ogundipe
C. E. Eckersley
Margaret Macaulay

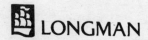 LONGMAN

Pearson Education Limited
Edinburgh Gate, Harlow,
Essex CM20 2JE,
England
and Associated Companies
throughout the world.

© Longman Group Ltd. 1983
All rights reserved; no part of this
publication may be reproduced, stored
in a retrieval system, or transmitted
in any form or by any means, electronic,
mechanical, photocopying, recording or
otherwise without the prior written
permission of the Publishers.

This edition first published 1983
Twenty-ninth impression 2010

Set in 10/12 Helvetica
Illustrations by Peter Edwards

Printed in Malaysia, PPSB

ISBN 978-0-582-60974-7

Preface

This is a new edition of *Brighter Grammar*. The continued popularity of this book, over the years, has shown that the necessity of grammar in the learning of a language is appreciated, not only by curriculum planners and teachers of English, but also by the students. School students like to have a handy revision book to reinforce lessons. Private students need a clear yet concise course to bring their competence in English to the level required, either to facilitate their further studies in professional fields, or for increased efficiency at their work places.

The success of *Brighter Grammar* has been due firstly to the fact that the subject is made completely understandable to even the least linguistically-minded student, by presenting it as simply and as clearly as possible. In the course only the essentials of grammar have been chosen, and these have been explained with the minimum of technical terms. Only those terms are taught which are necessary to understand the structure of the language and to aid the student's progress in all essential aspects, including composition.

Secondly, to show that the learning of grammar can be as enjoyable as that of any subject in the curriculum, the books have been made as lively and amusing as possible. Stories have been used as material for exercises and for "report" work in the composition lessons. The sentences in the exercises have been made as "real" as possible, and the four books brightened by lively drawings.

In addition, special attention has been paid to the exercises, which are graded, and nothing is asked of the student that he cannot answer from the lesson on which the exercise is based. Also, wherever necessary, the lessons in Book 2, Book 3 and Book 4 are preceded by a revision of the work covered in the earlier book or books.

This new edition will make *Brighter Grammar* even more useful than before. The course has been completely revised, and the improvements fall into three major categories:

1 Greater relevance to the African scene by the modification or even removal of culturally distant examples and stories, replacing them with usages, examples and stories more familiar to the African student.

2 Up-dating and modernising of the linguistic material to take into account the changes of idiom and usage which have made obsolete, or at least antiquated, certain items in the original edition. This up-dating is even more important to the African student than the editing or removal of references to a foreign culture. Any alert African student of English is aware that he is likely to come across references to a culture different from his own, and is therefore prepared to recognise and make efforts to understand them. But if periodic up-dating is not done, the student may find himself carefully learning some idiom or usage which, when used, will sound odd or outlandish to a comtemporary native English speaker.

3 Occasional expansion or the analysis of some grammatical points, so as to supply information which the original edition apparently assumed to be already known to the student. This filling in of gaps will be helpful to every student, especially those using the books on their own outside a classroom situation.

The authors therefore hope that *Brighter Grammar*, in this new and improved form, will continue to aid students, and give some relief to overburdened teachers, for many years to come.

Phebean Ogundipe
Lagos, Nigeria

Contents

Lesson

1. **Relative Pronoun** *Objective Case* 1
2. **Relative Pronoun** (2) 7
3. **Adverb Clauses** 13
4. **Clauses** 17
5. **Clauses** (2) 20
6. **Direct and Indirect Speech** *Questions* 25
7. **Indirect Speech** *Commands* 28
8. **Non-finites** *The Present Infinitive* 32
9. **The Present Infinitive** (2) 36
10. **Participles and Gerunds** 39
11. **Gerunds** 42
12. **The Subjunctive Mood** 46
13. **The Conditional** 49
14. **The Past Conditional** 52
15. **Defective Verbs** 55
16. **Defective Verbs** (2) *Must* 58
17. **The Peculiars Again** *Auxiliary Verbs* 61
18. **Auxiliary Verbs** (2) 64
19. **The Peculiars** *The Emphatic Form* 67
20. **The Peculiars** *Question Phrases* 70
21. **Short Answers** 74
22. **The Peculiars** *Additions to Remarks* 78
23. **A Word or Two on Punctuation** 82
    Goodbye 86

1 Relative Pronoun Objective Case

Revision. A clause is a sentence that does not make complete sense by itself. It depends on another sentence for its full meaning.

Clauses that depend on others for their meaning are called Subordinate Clauses. The chief clause in a sentence (usually the one on which the subordinate clauses depend) is called the Main Clause. A main clause and one or more subordinate clauses together make a Complex Sentence.

An Adjective Clause does the work of an adjective, i.e. it describes a noun. The adjective clause must go as near as possible to the noun it describes.

A Relative Pronoun does the work of a pronoun and of a conjunction. It stands instead of a noun and joins an adjective clause to another clause in a complex sentence.

If you are not quite sure about adjective clauses and relative pronouns, you would be wise to read again Lessons 17 and 18 in Book 3 because we are now going to have some rather more difficult examples of their use.

Here are some pairs of simple sentences. We will make them into complex ones by using relative pronouns:

Simple Sentences

1 (a) I liked the song. (b) Clara sang it.
2 (a) Here are the sheep. (b) My father bought them.
3 (a) Sing the song. (b) You sang it last night.
4 (a) Look at the big tree. (b) Baba cut it down yesterday.
5 (a) That is the boy. (b) I met him on Friday.
6 (a) I know that girl. (b) You spoke to her.
7 (a) Here is the man. (b) I was helped by him.
8 (a) This is the train. (b) I came by it.

Now here are those sentences joined together to make complex ones:
1 I liked the song which Clara sang.
2 Here are the sheep which my father bought.
3 Sing the song which you sang last night.
4 Look at the big tree which Baba cut down yesterday.
5 This is the boy whom I met on Friday.
6 I know the girl whom you spoke to. OR
   I know the girl to whom you spoke.
7 Here is the man whom I was helped by. OR
   Here is the man by whom I was helped.
8 This is the train which I came by. OR
   This is the train by which I came.

In most of these sentences, *that* can be used instead of *which* or *whom*. However, notice the alternative sentences in 6, 7, 8, where *that* can't be used.

Now look for a moment at those pronouns in the sentences (b); the pronouns *it, them, it, it, him, her, him, it*, which we replaced by relative pronouns when we made the complex sentences.

They are all in the objective case, either because they are objects of transitive verbs, or because they are governed by prepositions. So all the relative pronouns that replace them are in the objective case.

"Who" is the nominative case of the relative pronoun; "whom" is the objective case.

"Which" and "that" have the same forms for nominative or objective.

In the sentence:
   "This is the boy whom I met on Friday"
whom is the object of the verb *met*.

In the sentence:

"I know the girl to whom you spoke"

whom is the objective case governed by the preposition *to*.

You will notice that complex sentences 6, 7, and 8 are given in two ways, one with the preposition at the end of the sentence, the other with the preposition just before the relative pronoun.

You cannot use the second form with the relative pronoun *that*. It can only be used with *whom* or *which*.

Look at those complex sentences on page 2 again for a moment.

In sentence 1 the relative pronoun *which* stands instead of *song*; in No. 2 the relative pronoun *which* stands instead of *sheep*; in No. 3 the relative pronoun *which* stands instead of *song* and so on. All these relative pronouns are connected in meaning (or are "related") to a noun or pronoun in the main clause.

The word for which the relative pronoun stands is called the Antecedent.

"Antecedent" means "going before". So the antecedent of *which* in No. 1 is *song*; the antecedent of *which* in No. 2 is *sheep*; the antecedent of *whom* in No. 6 is *girl*.

There is one relative pronoun that doesn't have an antecedent. It is the relative pronoun *what*. It seems to be antecedent and relative pronoun all in one. It usually means "the thing which" or "that which".

Here are some examples:
>I brought him *what* he wanted.
>(I brought him *the thing which* he wanted.)

>This is *what* killed him.
>(This is *the thing which* killed him.)

>I'll now give you *what* I promised you.
>(I'll now give you *the thing which* I promised you.)

You will remember that sometimes the adjective clause divides the main clause. (Book 3, Lesson) What is the rule then, David?

DAVID I've remembered that all right. The rule is that the adjective clause must go next to the noun it describes.

TEACHER Good. Well, here are some examples of these "divided" complex sentences, with relative pronouns in the objective case:

Simple Sentences

1 (a) The boy is David Ekong.   (b) I questioned him about divided sentences.
2 (a) The girl is Arit Bassey.   (b) You spoke to her.
3 (a) The train was ten minutes late.   (b) I came by it.

Complex Sentences

1. The boy whom I questioned about divided sentences is David Ekong.
2. The girl whom you spoke to is Arit Bassey.
3. The train { which I came by OR } was ten minutes late.
   { by which I came }

Exercises

A Give the objective case of the pronouns:
I, you, he, she, it, we, they, who, which.
When is a pronoun in the objective case?

B Explain why "whom" and not "who" is used in the following sentences: *beacuse m is silent*
  1. I met a boy *whom* you know.
  2. Do you know the boy to *whom* I am referring?
  3. I know the girl *whom* you complained about.
  4. He is the brother of a boy *whom* I taught.
  5. There is the man *whom* I wrote the letter to.
  6. There is the man to *whom* I wrote the letter.
  7. Those children *whom* you saw studying grammar are in my class.
  8. The children to *whom* you spoke are learning grammar.
  9. The man with *whom* I was talking is the pilot of the plane.
  10. The man *whom* I got the information from is the pilot of the plane.

beacnz m is silent

C Join each of these pairs of simple sentences into a complex one by using a relative pronoun. Don't use "that" in sentences marked*.
  1. I liked the story. The man told it.
  2. * I liked the boy. You brought him to the house.
  3. That was an interesting story. You told it.
  4. * There is the boy. You saw him this morning.
  5. * Here is the girl. You spoke to her this morning.
  6. I have read the book. You told me about it.

7 There is the plane. I came to London by it.
8 * The pilot has flown ten thousand miles. I spoke to him.
9 * His brother is the navigator of the plane. I once met him in Beirut.
10 * These two men were both praised for bravery. I am proud to know them.

2 Relative Pronoun (2)

Omission

JOHN Please, sir, you have told us that the objective case of the relative pronoun *who* is *whom*. But *who* can also be an Interrogative Pronoun. Is the objective case of the Interrogative Pronoun also *whom*?

TEACHER Yes, it is. So you have sentences like this:

Whom did you see? (Object of the verb *see*.)
To whom was the letter addressed? (Governed by the preposition *to*.)

But you have probably noticed that we do not always speak as we write. In speaking, the rules of grammar are not always obeyed so strictly as they are in writing. Those sentences that I have given you would sound rather stiff and unnatural in speech and most people in ordinary conversation would say:

Who did you see?
Who was the letter addressed to?

We have something of that same feeling with *whom* as a relative pronoun, and so, in conversation, and sometimes in writing, **we very often leave out the relative pronoun when it is in the objective case**. So instead of:

This is the boy whom I met on Friday.
I know the girl whom you spoke to.
Here is the man whom I was helped by.
The girl whom you spoke to is Arit Bassey.

We say:

This is the boy I met on Friday.
I know the girl you spoke to.
Here is the man I was helped by.
The girl you spoke to is Arit Bassey.

The relative pronouns "which" and "that" when they are in the objective case can also be omitted, e.g.
> I liked the song Clara sang.
> Here are the sheep my father bought.
> This is the train I came by.

Possessive Case

Here are some more pairs of simple sentences which we will turn into complex ones by using a relative pronoun.

(a) I saw Taba.   (b) Her books were lost.

(a) This is the boy.   (b) Timi borrowed his bicycle.

(a) We read about the men.   (b) Their adventures thrilled the world.

(a) The boy has gone to London.   (b) His father came to see you.

You will notice that in the (b) sentences we haven't any pronouns, but we have the possessive words *her*, *his*, *their*. These words do the work of adjectives telling us more about the nouns *books, bicycle, adventures*; but they also indicate possession; *Her* books = *Taba's* books; *his* bicycle = *the boy's* bicycle; *their* adventures = *the men's* adventures, where the possessive form is shown by the *'s*. So these words are **Possessive Adjectives**.

We can make the pairs of simple sentences above into complex ones, by using *whose*, i.e. the Possessive form of the relative pronoun *who*, e.g.

I saw Taba *whose* books were lost.
This is the boy *whose* bicycle Timi borrowed.
We read about the men *whose* deeds thrilled the world.
The boy *whose* father came to see you has gone to London.

Note that the relative pronoun *whose* must go next to its antecedent. (See illustration below).

There is just one other rather small point about relative pronouns. *As* is often a relative pronoun when it is used after the words *same* and *such*.

Look at this complex sentence:

Meet me at the place that you did yesterday.

Quite clearly *that* is a relative pronoun. But if I put the word *same* in the main clause, then *that* is replaced by *as*, e.g.

Meet me at the *same* place *as* you did yesterday.

As is doing the same work as *that*. It is a relative pronoun. Or take this sentence:

I never buy the books that you do.

Here again, *that* is a relative pronoun. But put in *such*, and then *that* is replaced by *as*, e.g.

I never buy *such* books *as* you do.

Here are further examples of *as* being a relative pronoun after the words *such* or *same*.

He gave me the *same* answer *as* he gave you.

Yours is not the *same* book *as* mine is.

This is not *such* a good game *as* I expected.

I have never heard *such* good singing *as* I heard at the Festival concert.

Exercises

A Take out the relative pronouns *whom* or *which* and re-write the sentences putting the prepositions in their proper places (e.g. No. 8 = The chair he sat on had just been painted)
1. This is the train by which I came.
2. Do you know the boy to whom I am referring?
3. There is the man to whom I wrote the letter.
4. Who is the boy to whom you were talking?
5. This is the tree about which I told you.
6. The children to whom you spoke are learning grammar.
7. The man from whom I got the information is the pilot.
8. The chair on which he sat had just been painted.
9. The people with whom I live are very pleasant.
10. That is the box out of which he took the money.

B Join each of the following pairs of simple sentences into a complex one by using the relative pronoun *whose*.
1. (a) There is the man. (b) His dog bit me.
2. (a) The pilot has flown 10,000 miles. (b) I went in his plane.
3. (a) We travelled with a pilot. (b) His plane had flown round the world.
4. (a) The man works at a garage. (b) His dog bit me.
5. (a) Mary has invited us home. (b) Her mother teaches at Loyola.

C When is "as" used as a relative pronoun? Join these pairs of sentences by using the relative pronoun *as*:
1. (a) I never saw such bad work. (b) Victor has done it.
2. (a) This is the same story. (b) Kojo told it.
3. (a) Meet me in the same place. (b) You met me in it yesterday.
4. (a) He only does such work. (b) He is forced to do it.

D In the following sentences draw a line under each relative pronoun and put a square round each antecedent. If there is no relative pronoun or no antecedent put a mark like this ∧,

BRIGHTER GRAMMAR

e.g.   There is the ⬜man⬜ to <u>whom</u> I wrote the letter.

I liked the ⬜song⬜ ∧ Clara sang.

1 The burglar who stole the jewels has been caught.
2 I didn't like the people we met.
3 The boy whose dog was lost was very unhappy.
4 I don't know what I shall do.
5 There is the girl whose song you liked.
6 The girl who sang the song was Clara.
7 The picture which hung on the wall has fallen down.
8 I didn't read the book he sent me.
9 I explained what I wanted.
10 He sent me the same card as he sent you.

3 Adverb Clauses

Revision. An Adverb Clause does the work of an adverb, i.e. it tells more about a verb.

Clauses that tell "how" an action is done are Adverb Clauses of Manner; those that tell "when" an action is done are Adverb Clauses of Time; those that tell "where" an action is done are Adverb Clauses of Place.

You have had, so far, three kinds of adverb clauses: manner, time and place. But there are one or two other kinds of adverb clauses that you ought to know. They all tell something about the verb in the other sentence. The other sentence is usually the main clause; but sometimes, in long sentences with many clauses, an adverb clause may tell you more about the verb in another subordinate clause. And what they tell us enables us to decide what kind of adverb clause they are. Consider these groups:

Reason

The thief ran away *because he saw the policeman*.
WHY did he run away?
John passed his examination *because he worked hard*.
WHY did John pass his examination?
Because he hadn't worked hard, Victor didn't pass his examination.
WHY didn't Victor pass? What was the REASON for his failure?
Clauses that tell "why" something happened are Adverb Clauses of Reason.

Condition

The sentences in the next group are rather different.

Zakari will learn grammar *if he works hard*.
If the rain stops, I shall go for a walk.
We will help you, *if you need help*.
I cannot eat meat *unless it is well-cooked*.

These sentences tell us ON WHAT CONDITION Zakari will learn grammar, ON WHAT CONDITION I shall go for a walk, ON WHAT CONDITION I can eat meat. You will notice that *unless* = *if ... not*.

Clauses that express the condition on which an action was done, is done, or will be done, are called Adverb Clauses of Condition.

Concession

There is another kind of adverb clause that I think you ought to know. You will meet sentences like this:

Although Usman tried harder last term, his work is still not good enough.

The line of thought in the sentence is:

"I agree that Usman tried harder" or "I'll grant you that Usman tried harder" or "I'll concede the fact that Usman tried harder, but in spite of all that, his work is still not good enough".

So, because sentences like this "concede" something, they are called **Adverb Clauses of Concession**. Here are some further examples.

Though there was no hope of winning, the team played their hardest to the very end of the game.

He is a very active man, *though he is over eighty*.

Although Edosa got up early, he was late in arriving at school.

Although the work looks difficult, it is really quite simple.

Though I was telling him the truth, he still didn't believe me.

Clauses that "concede" or "grant" some fact in spite of which the statement in the Main Clause is made, are called Adverb Clauses of Concession.

Purpose

Finally here are some **Adverb Clauses of Purpose**.
They give the purpose for doing something.

LESSON 3   15

Chinua is working hard, *so that he may pass his examination.*

He locked the door, *so that he would not be disturbed.*

The thief disguised himself, *so that no one would recognize him.*

Exercises

Analyse the following complex sentences containing a main clause and an adverb clause. No. 1 is done for you. The "function" of a clause means the work it is doing.

Main Clause	Adverb Clause	Kind	Function
I need a hammer and nails	because I am going to repair the shed	Reason	Modifies the verb "need"

1 I need a hammer and nails, because I am going to repair the shed.
2 We couldn't play the match, because the field was too wet.
3 We shall come and see you, if we have a holiday.
4 Although it was rather wet, we played the match.
5 We shall play the match, even though it is rather wet.
6 We had to cancel the match, because it was so wet.
7 Mrs Buari locked the doors, so that thieves would not enter the house.

8 I will tell you the secret, if you won't tell it to anyone else.
9 If you will tell me the secret, I won't tell it to anyone else.
10 They went swimming, although the sea was very rough.
11 He told me the secret, so that I should help him.
12 Mrs Buari locked the doors, because she didn't want thieves to enter the house.

4 Clauses

MISS MACAULAY (teacher), MERCY, MARIAMA, LEILA, ENO, ELIZABETH.

MERCY Please, Miss Macaulay, do you ever have two subordinate clauses in a sentence? All the sentences you have given us so far have had one main clause and one subordinate clause, either an adjective clause, an adverb clause or a noun clause.

TEACHER Well, let us examine your question, Mercy. Here is a very simple sentence:

"The boy said something."

Now, Mariama, will you give us a noun clause instead of *something*.

MARIAMA I could say: "The boy said that he was hungry." Is that right?

TEACHER That is quite a good noun clause. As you give me additions I will write them on the blackboard. *The boy said* is the main clause; *that he was hungry* is a noun clause, object of *said*.

Now, Mercy, could you add an adjective clause?
First of all, what do adjective clauses do?

MERCY I think they do the work of an adjective, they describe nouns.

TEACHER Good. Well, there is only one noun (*boy*) in that sentence, so we need an adjective clause to describe *boy*. Who can give me one?

MERCY Well, if he was hungry he might be crying, so I will add: "The boy, *who was crying*, said that he was hungry."

TEACHER Well done, Mercy. But we haven't an adverb clause yet, have we? Leila, could you help us with an adverb clause?

LEILA Well, I think I could say HOW he was crying: and clauses that tell *how* something is done are adverb clauses of manner. So I will say:

"The boy, who was crying *as if his heart would break*, said that he was hungry."

TEACHER You have helped us a lot, Leila. Now could we add any more clauses. Eno?

ENO I think I could add an adverb clause of time. Would this be right?

"The boy, who was crying as if his heart would break, said, when I spoke to him, that he was hungry."

TEACHER That was good work, Eno. But I think we could add still one more clause. Will you try, Elizabeth?

ELIZABETH I can add an adverb clause of reason.

"The boy, who was crying as if his heart would break, said, when I spoke to him, that he was hungry, *because he had had no food for two days*."

TEACHER Well, Mercy, I think that has answered your question don't you?

MERCY Oh yes, Miss Macaulay. I see now that a complex sentence contains one main clause and one or more subordinate clauses.

TEACHER Yes. There are six clauses here. You can tell at once how many clauses there are in a complex sentence by noting how many finite verbs there are. Each finite verb represents a clause. If there are three finite verbs there will be three clauses. If there are ten finite verbs there will be ten clauses and so on.

Now let us take to pieces (or analyse) the sentence we have just put together. We will set it down like this.

CLAUSE	KIND
The boy said	Main Clause
who was crying	Adjective Clause describes "boy"
as if his heart would break	Adverb Clause (*Manner*)
when I asked him	Adverb Clause (*Time*)
that he was hungry	Noun Clause, object of "said"
because he had had no food for two days	Adverb Clause (*Reason*)

Exercises

Analyse these complex sentences in the same style as the one above.

A The pirates who had hidden the treasure on the island went back again because they thought that they could now remove it with safety.

B Rufai, though he had not previously answered any questions when the teacher asked him, now said that he knew the answer to this one because it was in the lesson that he had just read.

C When the teacher asked what part of speech a word was, John said, "I can tell you the answer, if you will give me a sentence in which the word is used."

5 Clauses (2)

TEACHER, RUFAI, CLARA, KOFI, JOHN, HASSAN.

RUFAI Please, sir, I have discovered an easy way of telling whether a clause is one of time or place and so on. This is my method: If it begins with *when* (a "time" word) it is a time clause; if it begins with *where* (a "place" word) it's a place clause; if it begins with *if* it's an adverb clause of condition; and if it begins with *who*, it's an adjective clause.

TEACHER Rufai, with most things in life there is a right way of doing something, and a wrong way. I'm afraid you have chosen the wrong way!

The wrong way to deal with clauses is to judge them by their first word. How do you know what part of speech a word is, Clara?

CLARA By the work it does, sir. (BOOK 1, LESSON 1)

TEACHER Correct. Now look at this, Kofi. Let us make a clause beginning with the word *where*. Here's a sentence:

The pirates went | where the treasure was hidden.

What kind of a clause is it, Kofi?

KOFI An adverb clause of place.

TEACHER Correct.
RUFAI But, please, sir, that was what I said!
TEACHER Listen, Rufai. Why is it an adverb clause, Hassan?
HASSAN Because it tells me about the verb *went*.
Clauses that tell us more about verbs are adverb clauses.
TEACHER Very good, Hassan. Now look at this sentence:

The pirates went to the island | where the treasure was hidden. |

What kind of a clause is *where the treasure was hidden*, John?

JOHN Please, sir, I think it is an adjective clause.
TEACHER But it begins with what Rufai calls a "place" word, *where*.
JOHN That doesn't matter. The clause tells us more about the noun *island*; and clauses that describe or tell more about nouns are adjective clauses.
TEACHER And you are quite right, John. I hope you are listening, Rufai! Now, here is another sentence:

The pirate told us | where the treasure was hidden. |

Clara, what kind of a clause is *where the treasure was hidden*?

CLARA I think it is a noun clause.
TEACHER But it begins with a "place" word, *where*. Rufai says it's an adverb clause.
CLARA No, sir, it isn't. In this case it is the object of the verb *told*. If you say, "The pirate told us WHAT?" the answer is, "Where the treasure was hidden." A clause that is the object of a verb is a noun clause.
TEACHER Quite right, Clara. Did you understand all that, Rufai?
RUFAI Yes, sir, I see now where I was wrong.
TEACHER In that sentence that John discussed, "The pirates went to the island where the treasure was hidden", *where* is the same as *on which*. We could write the sentence like this:
  "The pirates went to the island *on which* the treasure was hidden."
If you had seen it like that, you would have known at once that it was an adjective clause. The words *where* and *when* as used here are adverbs. But they are used to join adjective

clauses to another clause (as relative pronouns do), so they are called **Relative Adverbs**.

Now let us look at those other words that Rufai mentioned, *when, who* and *if*. Here are examples of clauses beginning with these words:

A I shouted with joy |when our school team won the prize.|
B I remember |when our school team won the prize.|
C I remember the day |when our school team won the prize.|
D Michael is the boy |who scored the winning goal.|
E I asked |who scored the winning goal.|
F Kwame asked me |if Michael had scored a goal.|
G We would all have cheered |if Garba had scored a goal.|

Now will you write down what kind of clause you think each one is. When you have tried for yourself, and not until then, look at the answers on page 24. Remember:

An Adjective Clause does the work of an adjective. It tells more about a noun.

An Adverb Clause does the work of an adverb. It tells more about a verb. There are Adverb Clauses of Time, Place, Manner, Reason, Condition, Concession.

A Noun Clause does the work of a noun. It is the subject or object of a verb.

Exercises

A Write out the following sentences, replacing the words in italics by *where* or *when*. What parts of speech are *when* and *where* as used in your sentences?
1 That is the house *in which* we stayed.
2 Do you remember the day *on which* he came to see us?
3 I think it was the day *on which* we had the heavy thunderstorm.
4 This is the place *at which* we were to meet.
5 Tomorrow is the day *on which* we get our birthday presents.

B What kind of clauses are the ones in italics?
   1. Tell me *where you are going for your holiday*.
   2. The place *where we stayed for our holiday* was right on the sea coast.
   3. I don't know *where we are going this year*.
   4. Come *where we are going for our holiday*.
   5. Do you know *where Shakespeare was born*?
   6. That is the house *where Shakespeare was born*.
   7. I don't remember *when Ike came to see me*.
   8. I think it was the day *when we had that heavy thunderstorm*.
   9. *If that was the day*, it can't be a year ago.
   10. I'll ask him *if he remembers the visit*.
   11. Tell me *who is coming to the party*.
   12. That's one of the boys *who is coming to the party*.

You can't please everybody

A man who owned a donkey was going on a journey with his son. Because the donkey was not big, only one of them could ride. *The other would have to walk*. The man decided that he would ride, and that his son would walk behind him.

The first person whom they met said, "Is it not strange that an adult man should ride although a weak little boy is walking?"

So that he might please him, the man got off the donkey and put his son in his place.

Soon another person passed them and said, "See how foolish this man is! A tired old man is walking, while his strong young son is riding!"

The man thought that he would please them if both he and his son rode, so he got onto the donkey and sat behind the boy.

But the next passer-by said, "You two are a heartless pair. Don't you know that you will kill this poor little donkey?"

The man was now confused, therefore father and son both got down and walked behind the donkey.

When another man passed he said, "Look at the world's greatest fools! Two people are going on foot, while their donkey has nothing to carry."

This finally taught the man sense. He told his son that he would stop trying to please everybody, because he who tries to please everybody will please nobody in the end. He said that he would ride until his son was tired from walking, and then he would get down and let the son ride until he was sufficiently rested.

Analyse all sentences, except the two in italics.

Answers to questions on page 22:
A An Adverb Clause of Time, going with the verb *shouted*.
B Noun Clause, object of the verb *remember*.
C Adjective Clause, telling more about the noun *day* (when = on which).
D Adjective Clause, telling more about the noun *boy*.
E Noun Clause, object of the verb *asked*.
F Noun Clause, object of the verb *asked*.
G Adverb Clause of Condition, going with the verb *would have cheered*.

Did you get them all right?

Direct and Indirect Speech Questions

Revision. In Direct Speech we have the exact words of the speaker. In Indirect Speech we have the words of a speaker reported indirectly by another speaker.

When a sentence changes from Direct Speech to Indirect Speech, it is introduced by a verb in the past tense (usually "said").

All verbs are changed from present tense to past tense.

Pronouns and possessive adjectives in the 1st person or 2nd person are changed to pronouns and possessive adjectives in the 3rd person.

You have already learned the difference between Direct Statements and Indirect Statements. (Book 3, Lesson 21). I now want to explain Direct and Indirect Speech where we have Questions.

If the Direct Speech is a question, the Indirect Speech is introduced by a word like "asked" instead of "said", e.g.

Direct Question: Mary said, "Are you hungry, Sefi?"
Indirect Question: Mary asked Sefi if she was hungry.
Direct Question: Leila said, "What do you want, Juliet?"
Indirect Question: Leila asked Juliet what she wanted.
Direct Question: TEACHER   Have you all understood me?
Indirect Question: The teacher asked the class if they had all understood him.
Direct Question: (JOHN to MARY)   Shall I close the window?
Indirect Question: John asked Mary if he should close the window.
Direct Question: (MOTHER to DAUGHTERS)   Who will do the work?
Indirect Question: The mother asked her daughters who would do the work.

Here are some further examples:

Direct Question	Indirect Question
EFUA (to Sule) Where are you going for your holidays?	Efua asked Sule where he was going for his holidays.
JULIUS (to shopkeeper) What is the price of that bicycle?	Julius asked the shopkeeper what the price of that bicycle was.
George said, "When will you get back from London, John?"	George asked John when he would get back from London.
George said, "How long does it take to get to London, John?"	George asked John how long it took to get to London.
Ben said, "Can you swim, John?"	Ben asked John if he could swim.
GEORGE (to teacher) Shall I finish my exercise at home, sir?	George asked the teacher if he should finish his exercise at home.
MARY May I have another cake, please?	Mary asked if she might have another cake.
ESSIE (to Gloria) Do you like my new hat?	Essie asked Gloria if she liked her new hat.

NOTICE

1 A Direct Question is in the "question form".
Verb before subject.
"Are you?" "Do you?" "Have you?" "Shall I?"

2 An Indirect Question is in the "statement form". Verb after subject.
"she was", "she wanted", "they had", "he should".

3 In Indirect Questions the question mark is omitted.

Notice, too, how in indirect speech the meaning may sometimes be ambiguous (i.e. not clear). Look at that last sentence:

"Essie asked Gloria if she liked her new hat."

"Her new hat" could mean "Essie's new hat" or "Gloria's new hat". To make the meaning unmistakable it is sometimes necessary to use the rather awkward form:

"Essie asked Gloria if she liked her (Essie's) new hat."

Exercises

A The following sentences are in Indirect Speech.
Give the direct words of the speaker. Don't forget the punctuation.

  1 Mrs Aidoo asked Ama if she was tired.
  2 Usman asked if they had taken his dog Bonzo for a walk.
  3 The hunter asked if they had heard the sound of wolves.
  4 The little girl asked if the baby had a name yet.
  5 The passenger inquired what time the train for Nairobi left.
  6 Kofi asked Peter if he had read *Treasure Island*.
  7 The stranger asked the way to the railway station.
  8 The lady asked George if he could swim.
  9 Dauda asked his mother if he might have another piece of cake.
  10 John asked Chinua if his exercise was correct.
(This is ambiguous. Give two answers).

B Turn the following from Direct Speech to Indirect Speech.

  1 MOTHER to EFUA "Have you finished your homework yet?"
  2 KOFI "Have you been using my toothpaste, Kwashie?"
  3 Mary said, "Is your new baby a boy or a girl, Mrs Dikko?"
  4 Elizabeth said, "Did Idayat feed the cat before she went out?"
  5 RUFAI'S MOTHER "Did you brush your teeth properly, Rufai?"
  6 The hunter said, "Do you hear the roar of a lion?"
  7 The hunter said, "Did you hear the roar of a lion?"
  8 VISITOR (to boy)   "Do you go to school every day?"
  9 JAMES "May I borrow your bicycle, John?"
  10 STRANGER to KOFI "Can you tell me where Mr Dikko lives?

7 Indirect Speech Commands

Here are some direct commands:
 "Open the window." "Let the man go."
 "Stay where you are."
Here are some that are not quite so "commanding"; they are polite requests rather than commands.
 "Open the window, please." "Try some of this kenki, it's very good." "Please don't make so much noise."

In Direct Commands and requests we use the imperative form of the verb (Book 3, page 42).

In Indirect Commands we don't use the imperative form; we use the infinitive.

We introduce the Indirect Command by some word like "told" or "ordered" (for commands), "asked" or "begged" (for polite requests). Here are some examples:

Direct Command (officer to soldier): Let (*imperative*) the man go.
Indirect Command: The officer ordered the soldier to let (*infinitive*) the man go.

Direct Command (teacher to boy): Open (*imperative*) the window.

Indirect Command: The teacher told the boy to open (*infinitive*) the window.

Direct Command: The officer said to the soldier, "Stay (*imperative*) where you are."

Indirect Command: The officer ordered the soldier to stay (*infinitive*) where he was.

Direct Command: Don't fire (*negative imperative*) the gun.

Indirect Command: The officer ordered the soldier not to fire (*negative infinitive*) the gun.

Direct request: Mary said, "Open the window please, John."

Indirect request: Mary asked John to open the window.

Direct request: (prefect to roomful of boys): "Please don't make so much noise."

Indirect request: The prefect begged the boys not to make so much noise.

Here are some further examples:

Direct Command	*Indirect Command*
TEACHER (to Amman) Go away!	The teacher ordered Amman to go away.
TEACHER (to Junaid) Clean the blackboard.	The teacher told Junaid to clean the blackboard.
The teacher said to Philip, "Come in."	The teacher told Philip to come in.
MOTHER (to Janet) Please don't eat all the cake.	Mother asked Janet not to eat all the cake.
OFFICER (to soldiers) Fire!	The officer commanded the soldiers to fire.
OFFICER (to sentry) Stay at your post until you are relieved.	The Officer told the sentry to stay at his post until he was relieved.
The teacher said to Fidelis, "Do that exercise correctly or you will be punished."	The teacher told Fidelis to do the exercise correctly or he would be punished.
TEACHER Don't waste your time, girls.	The teacher told the girls not to waste their time.

FARMER (to visitors) Please don't leave the gate open.	The farmer asked visitors not to leave the gate open.
Ahmed's father said, "Don't climb that tree in your new trousers, Ahmed."	Ahmed's father told him not to climb that tree in his new trousers.

If the Direct Speech is a command or a request, the Indirect Speech is introduced by "told", "ordered", "asked".

The Imperative in the Direct Speech is changed to Infinitive in the Indirect Speech.

"Don't" in the Direct Command becomes "not" in the Indirect Command.

Exercises

A Write the following as Indirect Commands or requests:
1. Teacher to Patrick: "Write that exercise out carefully."
2. Hunter to friend: "Shoot the wolf."
3. Officer to soldiers: "Bring the gun into position."
4. Mary said to John, "Open the box for me, please."
5. Mrs Ekong said, "Please sing at our party, Miama."
6. "Release the prisoners at once," said the officer to the sergeant.
7. The captain of the shipwrecked vessel said to the sailors, "Lower the boats."
8. Teacher to Edet: "Be careful; think before you answer."
9. Paul: "Read my exercise, John, and tell me if it is correct."
10. The pirate said to the prisoner, "Look at this map and show me where the treasure is hidden."

B Here is a short story containing Direct Statements, Questions and Commands. Rewrite it in Indirect Speech. Begin "The writer said that..."

Greedy Tortoise – Part 1

I will tell you a story of Tortoise. It was a time of famine, and Tortoise found some food which he wanted to eat secretly so as not to share it with his wife. So he went to the forest and asked a tree:

"Tree, can I sit under you to eat my food?"

"Yes, but you must give some to my children."

"How many have you?" asked Tortoise.

"Only three," replied Tree.

"Well, I can't spare food for three other eaters. I came here because there isn't enough for two of us."

Next he came to a stream and asked:

"Stream, can I sit on your bank to eat?"

"First, give some to my children," replied Stream.

"How many are they?" asked Tortoise.

"Only five," replied Stream.

"I just can't," said Tortoise. "I refused to give shares to the three children of Tree. How can I feed five streamlets?"

Non-Finites. The Present Infinitive

Revision (Book 2, pages 60–65). The parts of a verb that can stand alone to make a predicate are called *finite* verbs. The finite verbs are the simple present tense and the simple past tense.

The *non-finite* verbs are the present infinitive, the present participle and the past participle.

A finite verb changes its form in order to agree with its subject in number and person. The non-finites do not change.

When the present infinitive of a verb is used with another verb, it generally has "to" in front of it, e.g.

I want *to go* to London.

He asked me *to come* to his house.

Maria is able *to speak* French at last.

But after some verbs (shown here in italics) this "to" is left out.

Here are some examples. The words in the boxes are all present infinitives.

Maria *can* speak French.

I *shall* buy a new pen tomorrow.

I *didn't* finish my homework.

Will you lend me your book?

I think it *may* rain.

You *need* not do the work.

You *must* try harder.

TEACHER I said that after some verbs the *to* is left out. Do you notice which verbs they are, John?

JOHN Yes. They are the Peculiars. But I find it rather difficult to understand that *speak, buy, finish, lend*, etc, in those sentences really are infinitives.

TEACHER Well, I will put another verb, with more or less the same meaning, instead of the Peculiars; and you will find that the *to* is now used.

(*can*) Maria is able to speak French.
(*shall*) I am going to buy a new pen tomorrow.
(*didn't*) I failed to finish my homework.
(*will*) Are you willing to lend me your book?
(*may*) I think it is likely to rain.
(*need not*) You are not compelled to do the work.
(*must*) You will have to try harder.

JOHN Oh yes, I see that now. But do all the Peculiars take the infinitive without *to*?

TEACHER No. There are three that do not. They are: *ought, have* and *be*, e.g.

I ought to warn you about that.
You have to work hard to pass this examination.
I am to go there tomorrow at 9 o'clock.

There are also a few verbs in addition to the Peculiars, that don't take *to* with the infinitive. The chief ones are *make, let, hear, see, feel, watch*, e.g.

He *made* me do the work.
He forced me to do the work.

My father *let* me drive the car.
My father allowed me to drive the car.

I *heard* Ada play the piano.
We *saw* the bird fly onto the roof.
Isa *felt* his heart beat with excitement.
We *watched* it eat the crumbs.

34 BRIGHTER GRAMMAR

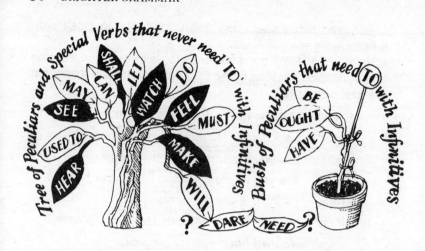

Finally, there are two, *dare* and *need*, which sometimes join the first group (infinitive with *to*), and sometimes join the second or Peculiars group (infinitive without *to*), especially in negatives and questions, e.g.

> I *need to* see my doctor.
> Yesterday Mina *dared to* contradict our teacher.
> *Need* I wait?
> *Dare* she call out loud?
> You *need* not do the work.
> He *dare* not go alone.

So, you must watch those two carefully. In fact, there are other times when they don't behave like Peculiars but like ordinary verbs, e.g.

> He doesn't dare!
> (Peculiar form: He dare not!)
> We don't need to go.
> (Peculiar form: We needn't go).

Exercises

A Copy out the following sentences and draw a line under every infinitive.

1 I want to write a letter.
2 I am going to write a letter.

LESSON 8   35

  3 John will write a letter also.
  4 Shall I write my letter now?
  5 Yes, you must write as soon as you can find time.
  6 Let me help you to write your letter.
  7 I don't want to make you write.
  8 I saw Mary write a very good letter.
  9 I know I don't write nearly as often as I ought to write.

B Put in a suitable infinitive in place of each of these dashes.
  1 I should like _____ you.
  2 Let me _____ them.
  3 You can't _____ without eyes.
  4 They mustn't _____ in the class.
  5 They were not allowed _____ in the class.
  6 Don't _____ my bicycle without permission.
  7 You ought not _____ my bicycle without permission.
  8 I want _____ home now.
  9 Let me _____ home now.

9 The Present Infinitive (2)

You have seen the present infinitive doing the work of a verb, but **the present infinitive sometimes does the work of a noun.**

A noun is often the subject or the object of a verb; and so is the infinitive. Look at these sentences:

The sight of Rufai's happy face gave me great pleasure.
"WHAT gave me great pleasure?"
... "The *sight* of Rufai's happy face." (*Noun*).

To see Rufai's happy face gave me great pleasure.
"WHAT gave me great pleasure?" ...
"*To see* Rufai's happy face." (*Infinitive*.)

Here are some more examples where the infinitive is the subject of the sentence.

To read a good book is one of the joys of life.
To make a mistake like that is very careless.
To learn grammar is not an easy thing.

In the following sentences the infinitive is the object of the sentence:

He promised *to help* me. ("He promised WHAT?")
We hope *to win* the match.
Akin tried *to open* the window.
My uncle has decided *to sell* his car.
The climbers failed *to reach* the top of the mountain.

The infinitive can even do the work of a noun clause. Look at these sentences. Sentences (a) contain noun clauses. Sentences (b) have more or less the same meaning but an infinitive has taken the place of a noun clause.

(a) He asked *if he could see Mr Buah*. (Noun clause)
(b) He asked to see Mr Buah. (Infinitive)
(a) Uncle Adjei promised *that he would give John a bicycle*. (Noun clause)
(b) Uncle Adjei promised to give John a bicycle. (Infinitive)

The Accusative Infinitive

A construction that you will probably meet in your reading is called the "accusative infinitive". Accusative is another word for objective.

Here are examples:

> I asked *him* (accusative) to come (infinitive) as soon as possible.
>
> He told *me* to go home.
>
> Wari taught *us* to swim.

After some verbs (those mentioned on page 33) the *to* is omitted.

> He made *me* show him where the treasure was hidden.
>
> They let *us* join in the game.
>
> We heard *the burglar* open the window, and saw *him* walk quickly upstairs.

We could say, then, that the infinitive is a "verb-noun".

It is like a noun because:
(a) it can be the subject,
(b) it can be the object of a verb.

It is like a verb because:
(a) it expresses an action,
(b) it can have an object, e.g.

	Infinitive	**Object of the Infinitive**
I am trying	to learn	grammar.
He likes	to read	a good book.

(c) it can be qualified by an adverb (as verbs are), e.g. To drive (*infinitive*) carefully (*adverb*) is better than to drive (*infinitive*) quickly (*adverb*).

I hope to see (*infinitive*) you soon (*adverb*).

Exercises

A Rewrite the following sentences using an infinitive construction instead of the words in italics:

1 I like *a walk* along the sea-shore.
2 The shipwrecked sailors were overjoyed *at the sight of* land.
3 *Truthfulness* is sometimes more difficult than *winning* a battle.
4 I was glad *at the sound of* his voice.
5 I should be sorry *if I heard* that you couldn't do this exercise.
6 Rufai was told *that he must not touch* the teacher's briefcase.
7 Mr Buah asked *if he could see* the headmaster.
8 I was very sorry *when I heard* that you had had an accident.
9 Niyi said that he did not expect *that he would get* all the exercise right.
10 The boys laughed *when they saw* the clumsy tricks of the magician's apprentice.
11 George asked *if he could borrow* John's bicycle.
12 The explorer said that he hoped *that he would reach* the North Pole.
13 If I don't prepare my work *it is certain that* the teacher *will ask* me a question that I can't answer.

10 Participles and Gerunds

Revision (Book 2, pp. 40–46). The form of the verb that ends in *-ing* is called the Present Participle. The present participle is used with the verb *to be* to form the Continuous Tenses.

The past participle of weak verbs is made by adding *d, ed* or *t* to the stem of the verb. The past participle of strong verbs is made by changing the vowel (Book 2, pp. 6–69). The past participle is used with the verb *to have* to form the perfect tenses (Book 3, pp. 15, 21, 23, 38).

There is another part of the verb, besides the present infinitive, that is partly a noun and partly a verb. It always ends in *-ing*; e.g. *running, reading, talking*, etc. It is called the **Gerund**.

DAUDA   But, sir, you said the present participle always ends in *-ing*.

TEACHER   I did, and it does.

DAUDA   Well, in that case, as they both look exactly the same, how can we tell a present participle from a gerund?

TEACHER   How do you always tell what part of speech a word is?

DAUDA   By the work it does.

TEACHER   Exactly! Now listen and we will get this matter clear.

Here are some **Present Participles**.

> The *running* horse galloped down the road.
> Listen to that *singing* bird.

What work is *running* doing there, Irene?

IRENE   It is telling us about the noun *horse*.

TEACHER   Correct. And what work is *singing* doing there?

IRENE   It is telling us about the noun *bird*.

TEACHER   Quite right. And what do we call words that tell more about nouns?

IRENE Adjectives.

TEACHER Very good. But these words *singing* and *running* are also partly verbs; they are part of the verbs *to sing* and *to run*. They are called participles. *Singing* and *running* are present participles. The **Past Participles** do exactly the same work. Look at these examples:

> There was some *broken* glass on the road.
> Those are *stolen* goods.
> Brightly *coloured* pictures hung on the wall.

Broken, stolen, coloured are parts of the verbs *to break, to steal, to colour*. They are past participles. Here they are doing the work of adjectives in telling more about *glass, goods*, and *pictures*.

So, you see, a participle does something of the work of a verb and something of the work of an adjective. If we were doing mathematics we might write it like this:

$$\text{PARTICIPLE} = \text{VERB} + \text{ADJECTIVE}$$
$$P = V + A$$

A participle is partly a verb and partly an adjective.

Exercises

A Give the present participle and the past participle of the following verbs: (one has two past participle forms – give both.)
walk, choose, dig, fight, forgive, freeze, hang, ride, ring, rise, run, begin, break, buy, come, tie, lay, write, fall, fly.

B What work does a participle do?

C In what tenses are present participles used? (Book 2, pages 40–43 and Book 3, pages 21, 36)

D What verbal uses have past participles?

E Write down the present participles in the following sentences and show that they are being used as adjectives. You can do this by pointing out the noun that each one qualifies.

    1 I know the missing word in that sentence.
    2 The hero was welcomed home by cheering crowds.
    3 I don't like to see singing birds in cages.
    4 The boy took a flying leap into the water.
    5 The man walking down the street sang as he walked.
    6 The man led a dancing bear on a chain.
    7 I was kept awake by a barking dog.
    8 The rushing wind roared in our ears.
    9 The teacher told us an amusing story.
   10 The boy running out of the house is Audu.

11 Gerunds

In the last lesson we looked at the present participle, the part of the verb that ends in *-ing* and is partly a verb and partly an adjective.

Now look at these sentences:
1. *Running* is my favourite sport.
2. *Seeing* is *believing*.
3. *Crying* won't help matters.
4. *Speaking* a language every day is the best way of *learning* it.
5. I like to hear good *singing*.
6. Our house needs *painting*.
7. I hate *losing* my temper.
8. I don't remember *seeing* you before.
9. You won't do any good by *crying*.
10. The girl was praised for *doing* her work neatly.
11. Minji is fond of *swimming* in deep water.
12. You can't live without *eating*.

What work is being done by *running, seeing, crying, speaking* (sentences 1, 2, 3, 4), Kofi?

KOFI They are all names of actions. They are subjects of verbs. They are doing the work of nouns.

TEACHER Quite right, Kofi.
Now look at sentences 5, 6, 7, 8. What work is being done by *singing, painting, losing, seeing*, Shehu?

SHEHU I think they are objects of verbs. They are doing the work of nouns.

TEACHER Very good, Shehu. Now, Mary, look at sentences 9, 10, 11, 12. What do you notice about the words *crying, doing, swimming, eating*?

MARY They are all the names of things. They are like nouns.

LESSON 11 43

TEACHER   Quite true. In fact in some of them you could put an ordinary noun instead of the word ending in *-ing*, for example:

  9 You won't do any good by *tears* (crying).
10 The girl was praised for *neatness* (doing her work neatly).
12 You can't live without *food* (eating).

Did you notice too that they were all governed by prepositions –

> *of* swimming
> *by* crying
> *without* eating
> *for* doing, etc?

and you know that prepositions generally govern nouns. (Book 1, page 71) So quite plainly these words, as used in these sentences, are partly nouns.

But they are also partly verbs. They express an action. Besides, if they are formed from transitive verbs they take objects, just as verbs do, e.g.

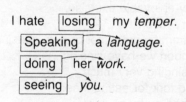

I hate losing my *temper*.
Speaking a *language*.
doing her *work*.
seeing *you*.

GERUND   **PRESENT PARTICIPLE**

These words are partly verbs and partly nouns. They are not participles. They are **Gerunds**. So besides the "participle formula" P = V + A, let us put the "gerund formula" G = V + N.

A gerund is the part of a verb ending in -ing that is partly a verb and partly a noun.

A gerund can be the subject or the object of a verb or it may be governed by a preposition.

If a gerund is formed from a transitive verb it can take an object.

Exercises

A What is the meaning of G = V + N?

B As a gerund and a present participle are exactly the same in appearance, how can you tell which is which?

C Point out the gerunds in the following sentences and give the function of each (i.e. the work each is doing). Say whether it is the subject of a verb, object of a verb or governed by a preposition.
  1 Swimming is a very enjoyable exercise.
  2 I like swimming very much.
  3 John is fond of swimming but Janet prefers dancing.
  4 Every Friday afternoon we have singing.
  5 Rufai doesn't like singing very much.
  6 We use a knife and fork for eating meat.
  7 You will only succeed by trying hard.
  8 Mr Ekong likes gardening; but he doesn't like cutting the grass.
  9 I don't want to force you into doing something against your will.
  10 David hates getting up early in the morning.

D Say which of the words in italics are gerunds and which are present participles.
  1 The *retreating* army took up new positions.
  2 They hated *retreating* before the enemy, but by *retreating* they avoided capture.
  3 They were *retreating* because they had lost their heavy guns.
  4 Mr Popo is *working* in his garden.

5 By *working* hard he hopes to get the garden ready for *sowing* seeds.
6 "There was a *rustling* that seemed like a *bustling*,
Small feet were *pattering*, wooden shoes *clattering*.
Little hands *clapping* and little tongues *chattering*.
Out came the children *running*.
All the little boys and girls,
With *sparkling* eyes and teeth like pearls,
Tripping and *skipping*, ran merrily after
The wonderful music with *shouting* and laughter."
(From *The Pied Piper of Hamelin* by Robert Browning.)

12 The Subjunctive Mood

Revision. Mood is the form of the verb that expresses the manner in which an action is done.

The Indicative mood is used to make statements and ask questions.

The Imperative mood is used to give orders or make requests.

The **Subjunctive mood** is used to express a wish, or a prayer that something may be, e.g.

God help you!

This means "I hope and pray that God will help you."

Very often the subjunctive is expressed by using one of the Peculiars, *may* (*might*), e.g.

Long *may* she reign.

A happier time is coming. *May* I live to see it.

He wished that he *might* see happier times.

The subjunctive has also another use; it is used in conditional clauses implying a negative.

JOHN   Please, sir, I don't understand what "implying a negative" means.

TEACHER   Well, let me explain it to you.

Suppose, John, I say to you, "If I were captain of a ship I'd take you on a voyage round the world." What do you know about me from that remark? Do you know that I am the captain of a ship, or that I am not?

JOHN   I know that you are not a captain of a ship.

TEACHER   How do you know?

JOHN   Anyone could gather that from the remark, "If I were..."

TEACHER   Yes, I quite agree. The remark "implies" that I am not the captain.

Now, Helen, here is a sentence for you. "If Ada were here, she would help me with my work." From that sentence could you say whether Ada is here or not?

HELEN She is not here.

TEACHER But *not* is a negative word and I don't see any "*not*" or any other negative word in my sentence.

HELEN No, there isn't a negative but you gather the negative idea from the sentence.

TEACHER Oh, I see. You mean that the negative is implied, but not actually expressed. Let us take another sentence or two.

"If I were in your place I would work harder."

What is the implied negative, Musa?

MUSA That you are not in my place.

TEACHER Right.

"I would lift the box if it were possible." Christie, what is the implied negative?

CHRISTIE The implied negative is... "but it is not possible".

TEACHER Now, I think you all understand the point so I will repeat what I said at first.

The Subjunctive mood is used in Conditional Clauses implying a negative.

And I want you to look again at the verbs in these conditional clauses.

If I *were* captain....

If Ada *were* here....

If I *were* in your place....

If it *were* possible....

With the pronoun "I" (*1st person singular*) and "he" (*3rd person singular*) you generally have the verb "*was*", e.g. I *was* surprised, Hassan *was* at home; It *was* your fault.

Were is generally used only for the plural (e.g. *we were, you were, they were*).

But in the four unfinished sentences above, **the "were" is not plural, but Subjunctive.**

That one construction *If I were, If you were, If he were*, etc., is practically the only example we have in modern spoken English of the subjunctive mood expressed by the form of the verb.

Now I think we can complete the definition with which the lesson opened.

CONDITIONAL CLAUSE

IMPLIED NEGATIVE

If I were a captain.

I am not the captain.

If Ada were here.

Ada is not here.

If I were in your place.

I am not in your place.

If it were possible.

It is not possible.

The Subjunctive mood is used to express a wish or a prayer.

The Subjunctive mood is also used for a condition implying a negative.

Exercises

A What are the uses of the Subjunctive mood?

B What are the implied negatives in the following sentences?
 1 If you were Titus what would you do?
 2 If I were a bird I wouldn't sing in a cage.
 3 If Kassim were here he would tell us the answer.
 4 If I were the King I'd make you my Queen.
 5 "If you were the only girl in the world and I were the only boy...." (*Popular song.*)

What mood is *were* in all those sentences?

13 The Conditional

In the lesson on adverb clauses, you met some adverb clauses of Condition, clauses like these:

If Zakari works hard, he will learn grammar.

I will help him, *if he asks me*.

These clauses simply mean: "If Zakari works he will learn; if he doesn't work he won't learn."

"If he asks me I will help him; if he doesn't ask me, I won't help him."

Zakari has the choice between "working" and "not working". He has the choice between "asking" and "not asking". These are what we call "open conditions". We don't know yet what will happen: Zakari may work hard, or he may not. Similarly, he may ask for help, and again he may not.

Notice the construction in an "open condition".

In the Condition Clause we have the Simple Present Tense. In the Principal Clause we have the Simple Future Tense.

But there is another conditional form. Here are some examples set side by side with "open conditions".

A	B
If Zakari works hard he will learn grammar.	If Zakari worked hard he would learn grammar.
I will help him if he asks me.	I would help him if he asked me.
He will do the work if he has time.	He would do the work if he had time.
I shall go for a walk if the rain stops.	I would go for a walk if the rain stopped.

What will you do if I give you the choice?
We will help you if you need help.
*I shall speak if I am sure of the answer.

What would you do if I gave you the choice?
We would help you if you needed help.
*I would speak if I were sure of the answer.

*Strictly grammatically speaking, "shall" ought to be changed to "should" but in modern usage "would" is becoming more acceptable, and "should" has been left to the more common meaning of "ought". Imagine the confusion of a sentence like: "Strictly, we should say 'should', but if we did that, we should only be confusing you, which we shouldn't do." Compare that with, ". . . We would only be confusing you, which we shouldn't do."

TEACHER Do you notice anything about all those sentences marked **B**, John? Look at the first one for example.

JOHN Well, the present tense *works* has changed to the past tense *worked* and *will learn* has changed to *would learn*.

TEACHER Yes, that's quite true, but do you see anything else? Think back to our conversation in the last lesson.
When I say "If Zakari worked hard he would learn grammar" what do I imply?

KWESI Oh, I see it; you imply that he doesn't work hard. It's an implied negative! It's like the subjunctive!

TEACHER Exactly. In fact one of the ways of showing the subjunctive is by using *should* and *would*. And all the other sentences are the same.
"I would help him if he asked me" implies "but he doesn't ask me".
"He would do the work if he had the time" implies "but he hasn't the time".
and so on.

The **A** sentences are Open Conditions; the **B** sentences are Subjunctive Conditionals.

Unlike the Open Conditions, we already know that something has happened, or rather, has not happened.

Where there is an implied negative we use the Subjunctive Conditional.

Exercises

A Which of the following are Open Conditions and which are Subjunctive Conditionals?
1 If it is not wet tomorrow we will come.
2 If I saw him I would speak to him.
3 I would play football if you asked me.
4 If you are right, then I am wrong.
5 If you gave that answer you would be wrong.
6 If he spoke to me I would speak to him.
7 If he asked for money would you give him any?
8 Will you give him money if he asks for it?
9 If it were not so wet we would play football.
10 If he feels hungry he will eat his dinner.

B Change the following from Open Conditions to Subjunctive Conditionals:
1 If you ask me I will play football.
2 I shall speak to him if he speaks to me.
3 If he listens to what I say he won't make silly mistakes.
4 If the sun comes out the rain will soon stop.
5 He will open the box if he can find the key.
6 If he feels hungry he will eat his dinner.
7 If I begin the work, he will finish it.
8 If you feed the cat properly it will soon be well.

14 The Past Conditional

TEACHER Do you remember, when we were studying these sentences in the last lesson:

Open Condition	Subjunctive Conditional
If Zakari works hard he will learn grammar.	If Zakari worked hard he would learn grammar.
We will help you if you need help.	We would help you if you needed help.
He will do the work if he has time.	He would do the work if he had time.

I asked John if he noticed anything about them. His answer was that in the Subjunctive Conditionals the past tense *worked* was used instead of the present tense *works*, and *would learn* was used instead of *will learn*.

Well, the funny thing is that though we use a *past* tense, the meaning is really a *present* one.

They mean:

...if he worked hard NOW...(but he doesn't work hard NOW).

...if you needed help NOW...(but you don't need help NOW).

...if he had time NOW...(but he hasn't time NOW).

In other words all these sentences are **Present Subjunctive Conditionals**.

We can have Subjunctive Conditionals in the past tense also. Here is how we would express the Past Conditional. As you will see we use the Past Perfect tense and *would have*.

Zakari *would have* learned grammar, if he *had worked* hard (but he didn't work hard – IN THE PAST – and he didn't learn IN THE PAST).

We *would have* helped you if you *had needed* help (...but you didn't).

He *would have* done the work if he *had had* time (...but he didn't have time.)

Here are some further examples of these three constructions to help you to understand them.

Open Condition. If the master pays him properly the workman will work well.

Present Conditional. If the master paid him properly the workman would work well.

Past Conditional. If the master had paid him properly the workman would have worked well.

Open Condition. If these stamps are genuine they will be worth a lot of money.

Present Conditional. If these stamps were genuine they would be worth a lot of money.

Past Conditional. If these stamps had been genuine they would have been worth a lot of money.

Open Condition. If I know what you want I will buy you a present.
Present Conditional. If I knew what you wanted I would buy you a present.
Past Conditional. If I had known what you wanted I would have bought you a present.

In the Past Conditional in the Condition Clause we have the past perfect tense; in the Main Clause we have "would" with "have" and a past participle.

This summary of this rather difficult matter may help you:

		Main Clause	Condition Clause
	OPEN CONDITION	he will learn	if he works (*Simple Present*)
SUBJUNCTIVE	PRESENT CONDITIONAL	he would learn	if he worked (*Simple Past*)
	PAST CONDITIONAL	he would have learned	if he had worked (*Past Perfect*)

Exercises

A Turn these sentences (a) into Present Subjunctive Conditional, (b) into Past Subjunctive Conditional. The first one is done for you.

1 If you do that you will be all right.
   (a) If you did that you would be all right.
   (b) If you had done that, you would have been all right.
2 If the cat is hungry I will give it some food.
3 If it rains the party will be spoiled.
4 If you leave immediately you will catch the train.
5 Kofi will pass his examination if he works.
6 I will give him the money if I see him.
7 If you drink that it will kill you.
8 The boy will post your letter if you give it to him.

15 Defective Verbs

There are some verbs (and as you might expect, they are Peculiars *can, may, shall, will, must, ought.*) that have certain parts missing. For that reason they are called defective verbs.

CAN

Can is the first of them. It has only two forms; the present *can* and the past *could. Can* means *to be able.* For example you can say:

Can you speak Swahili? OR
Are you *able* to speak Swahili?

Tamuno *could* swim when he was six years old. OR
Tamuno *was able* to swim when he was six years old.

Can has no future tense or past participle or infinitive, so instead it uses some form of *to be able*, e.g.

Future. I *shall be able* to do this exercise now that you have explained it.

Past Participle. Tamuno *has been able* to swim for six years.

Infinitive. I hope *to be able* to come to the party tonight.

MAY

Another defective verb is *may*. Here again there are only two forms, *may* and *might*.

May is often used to ask permission, e.g.

KOFI   "*May* I borrow your bicycle, Timi?"
AFI AND MARY   "*May* we go into your shop, Mr Dina?"

Quite often, as a matter of fact, we use *can* to ask permission, e.g.

Can I borrow your bicycle?
Can we go into your garden?

But "I can" really means "I am able to". "I may" means "I am allowed to". You will see the difference perhaps in this little conversation.

NEW STUDENT   "*Can* I eat in the dormitory?"
PREFECT   "You *can*, Charles, but you *may* not."

If we put these sentences into the past tense we get the form *might*, e.g.

Kofi asked if he *might* borrow Timi's bicycle.
Afi and Mary asked if they *might* go into Mr Dina's shop.
The new student asked the prefect if he could eat.
The perfect said that he could but that he *might* not.

For the missing parts of *may* we do as we did with *can*, i.e. use another verb (generally *allow* or *let*), e.g.

Present Tense.   Kofi *may* borrow my bicycle.
Past Tense.   Timi said Kofi *might* borrow his bicycle.
Past Participle.   Timi *has allowed* Kofi to borrow his bicycle.
   Timi *has let* Kofi borrow his bicycle.
Future.   Timi *will allow* Kofi to borrow his bicycle.
   Timi *will let* Kofi borrow his bicycle.
Continuous Tense.   I *am allowing* Kofi to borrow my bicycle.
   I *am letting* Kofi borrow my bicycle.

Sometimes *may* (might) expresses another meaning, that is, possibility.

You will see that meaning in these examples:

MARY AND AFI   We want to have a picnic this afternoon, Mother. Do you think it is going to rain?
MOTHER   Well, it *may* rain; there are some clouds in the sky. But the sun *may* come out and clear them away.

And here's what the girls said the next morning talking of their picnic:

"Before we went for our picnic we asked mother if she thought it *might* rain. She said it *might* because there were clouds in the sky, but she hoped the sun *might* come out and clear the clouds away. And I'm glad to say it did and we had a lovely picnic."

May and *might* are also used to form the subjunctive. (See page 46).

Exercises

A Why are *may* and *can* called Defective Verbs?

B What are the two meanings of: "I may go with you to the cinema"?

C What is the difference in meaning between "I can swim" and "I may swim"?

D *May* and *might* are used to form the Subjunctive. Give an example.

E In the following sentences replace "can" ("could") by the necessary "to be able" form:
1. Tamuno can swim well.
2. I could hear every word you said.
3. I couldn't hear a word you said.
4. Kwame can lift that heavy box.
5. Sefi couldn't lift that heavy box.
6. We can't do all these exercises in five minutes.
7. I can just hear what he says.
8. I could just hear what he said.
9. What time tomorrow can I see you? ("*Tomorrow*" *suggests a future time.*)
10. Can you see me tomorrow?

F Turn the following sentences (a) into the Simple Past Tense, (b) into the Future Tense. Add any necessary "time" expressions:
1. He can stay here for an hour.
2. You can do this exercise quite easily.
3. I can write to him because I have his address.
4. I can't write to him because I haven't his address.
5. We can't understand him because he speaks English so badly.

16 Defective Verbs (2) Must

The verb *must* has only that one form, as does *ought*. It has no infinitive, no past tense, no future tense and no participle. But first let us look at its meaning.

Its main meaning suggests a **command** or an **obligation**, e.g.
   Tony *must* finish his work before he goes home.
   You *must* write your exercise neatly.
   I *must* try hard to understand this lesson.

Or in the negative:
   You *mustn't* play football in the street.
   People *must not* try to feed these animals.
   I *mustn't* go to sleep during the grammar lesson.

There is another meaning that suggests not compulsion but rather **what seems reasonable**, e.g.
   You have worked hard all day, you *must* be tired.
   Bitrus *must* be pleased that he has passed his examination.
   If Olu left here at four o'clock, he *must* be home by now.

Negative

For the negative of this second meaning, the use of "must" is going out of practice because of the danger of confusing it with command or obligation. Therefore, in modern usage, the negative of "Mr Atta must have received my letter by now" would be "Mr Atta can't have received my letter, or he'd have replied by now", or even: "It must be that Mr Atta hasn't yet received my letter..." which is a little longer but perfectly acceptable.

Similarly, the negative of "The Dinas must be at home now" would be: "The Dinas can't be at home, otherwise someone would have answered the telephone"; or "It must be that the Dinas aren't at home, otherwise someone would have answered the phone."

A peculiar thing about the negative of *must* is that there are two negatives according to the meaning. Sometimes the opposite of must is *must not* (*mustn't*), and sometimes it is *need not* (*needn't*). Here is a short conversation to illustrate this:

The Party

ALIU We are having a party at our house tomorrow, Mary. It begins at four o'clock. Will you come?

MARY Thank you very much. I should like to come but we have school in the afternoon. *Must* I come at four o'clock?

ALIU Oh no, you *needn't* come at four, but you *mustn't* be too late or all the best food may be gone.

MARY But I *must* go home first to put on another dress.

ALIU Oh, you *needn't* do that. You will be late if you do. The dress you are wearing is very nice.

MARY Oh yes, I *must* change my dress, but you *needn't* worry, I shan't be very late. I'll be there by half-past four.

Use "mustn't" when the meaning suggests a command.
Use "needn't" when the meaning is "it is not necessary".

Here is one more example.

Affirmative.   You *must* give the man five shillings.

Negative. (1)   You *mustn't* give the man five shillings (command).

Negative. (2)   You *needn't* give the man five shillings (it isn't necessary but you can do as you please, give it or not give it).

We can't use *shall* or *will* with *must*. So to express the future we use *have to*, e.g.

1) I shall *have to* see the dentist tomorrow.
2) They will *have to* run if they want to catch the train.

We can of course say:

3) I must see the dentist tomorrow.

But if we want to use the auxilliaries *shall* and *will* in our sentence, "shall have to" or "will have to" is needed to express the idea of *must*, as in the sentences 1) and 2) above.

What about the past tense? Unlike sentence 3) above, where

we used *must* with *tomorrow*, we can never use *must* with *yesterday* or in any past tense construction. Instead, we use *had to*, e.g.

I *had to* go to the dentist yesterday about my bad tooth.

They *had to* run to catch the train.

But the negative "did not have to" only carries the meaning of "needn't" and not the command meaning of "must not". For "must not" in the past tense, we have to use expressions like "... was forbidden to" or "... was not to", e.g.

Susan must not walk alone at night

becomes, in the past tense,

1) Susan was forbidden to walk alone at night OR
2) Susan (was told that she) was not to walk alone at night.

Exercises

A What are the two main meanings of *must*? Give examples of each.

B Put in "mustn't" or "needn't" in the blank spaces. Choose the one that seems to you the more suitable.

1 You _____ do the work this evening; tomorrow will be soon enough.
2 I told him that he _____ say those silly things.
3 You _____ sit there in your wet clothes; you will catch cold if you do.
4 They _____ do all the exercises; it will be sufficient if they do four of them.
5 We _____ go just yet; our train doesn't leave for an hour.

C Put the following sentences into the Simple Past Tense. Make any necessary alterations to "time phrases".

1 I must give an answer at once.
2 We must clear away the bush before we can get to the gate.
3 I must read to the end of the story because I want to see who gets the treasure.
4 Lydia must not open the box of chocolates until her sister comes home.
5 They must leave the house because the new owner wants to move in.

17 The Peculiars Again Auxiliary Verbs

Revision (Book 2, pages 50–58). There are twelve Peculiars (and their various parts):- *be, have, can, do, shall, will, may, must, need, ought, dare, used to*.

They are the only verbs that form their negative by adding *not* only.

They are the only verbs that form their interrogative by inversion, and the only ones that use contracted forms. They all (except *have, be, ought*) are followed by the infinitive without *to* (see Lesson Eight).

You have already seen some of the work that the Peculiars do. They like to be helpful. For example, *do* helps other verbs to form the interrogative.

Do you like chocolate?
Did you offer Mary some chocolate?

It helps, too, to form the negative, e.g.

I *do* not like chocolate.
I *did* not offer Mary any chocolate.

Other peculiars help to form tenses, e.g.

I *have eaten* my chocolate (Present Perfect Tense).
I *had eaten* it before you came (Past Perfect Tense).
I *was eating* chocolate during the lesson (Past Continuous Tense).
Aliu *is eating* some now (Present Continuous Tense).
I *shall keep* this chocolate until after the lesson. (Future Tense).
I *shall have eaten* it all by tomorrow (Future Perfect Tense).

Others again help verbs to form the Passive Voice

The thief *will be caught*.
The thief *was caught*.
The thief *has been caught*.

May and *might*, *should* and *would* help to form the Subjunctive mood and the Conditional, e.g.

Long *may* you live (Subjunctive)

If only I *might* go to London, how happy I *should* be (Subjunctive).

Ada *would* learn grammar if she worked hard (Conditional).

I *would be* happy if I could go to London (Conditional).

Because these verbs (*be, have, do, will, shall*, etc.) help other verbs they are called auxiliary or "helping" verbs.

Exercises

A What are auxiliary verbs?

B Give examples of an auxiliary verb:
  1 forming a negative,   2 forming an interrogative,
  3 forming a tense,   4 forming the passive voice,
  5 forming the Subjunctive.

C Here is a short story:

Greedy Tortoise – Part 2

Finally Tortoise came to a big, smooth rock.

"Rock, may I sit on you to eat my food?"

"Yes, if you will agree to give some to my children."

"How many are they?" asked Tortoise, hoping that Rock would say there were just two or three.

"Only seven, and they have gone out to play."

By now, Tortoise was so hungry, and he had come so far, that he could go no farther.

"How can I share with seven rocklets when I could not even give a little to my wife?" he said to himself. "But I am going to die of hunger if I don't find somewhere to sit and eat." So reluctantly he placed seven small portions on the rock, and sat down to eat.

When he had finished, and was licking his fingers, he looked longingly at the seven portions on the rock and thought: "These are too big; a small rocklet cannot eat this much. I shall take a little of each portion." He did so, but the remaining portions still looked too big to his greedy eyes, so he kept on reducing them until there were only seven very small portions left.

"I might as well eat the rest," he said to himself. "One tiny morsel is too small for a growing rocklet. Even I can hardly see them, they are so small!"

So he ate everything. Then tried to get up, but found that he couldn't. To punish him for not keeping his promise to leave food for the children, the rock had stuck itself firmly to his backside, and made him a prisoner.

Pick out all the auxiliaries, and say what work each one is doing.

18 Auxiliary Verbs (2)

We will begin this lesson with a "rule". Here it is:
   The auxiliary verbs are never used alone. They are always used with a non-finite or another verb, e.g.

(will)   I will **help** (*infinitive*) you.
(can)   He can **speak** (*infinitive*) French.
(do)   I don't **know** (*infinitive*) your friend.
(are)   We are **learning** (*present participle*) grammar.
(have)   We have **learned** (*past participle*) about non-finites.

(For non-finites, see Book 2, pages 60–73)

JOHN   But, please, sir, what about the verb *do* in this sentence? The gardener *did* his work well.
Did is used alone there; there isn't any non-finite of another verb.

TEACHER   Well done, John. I was hoping someone would bring up that point. The explanation is this. Four of the Peculiars (*be, have, do* and *need*) "lead a double life". Sometimes they are Peculiars and act like Peculiars, and sometimes they are ordinary verbs and act like all the other verbs. When they are ordinary verbs they don't need a non-finite to complete them.

They are normal verbs and can make a predicate by themselves. Let me show you examples.

(1) *be, have, do, need*, as auxiliary verbs:
   I *am* teaching grammar.
   I *have* taught grammar.
   Do you understand this lesson?
   You *needn't* feel worried, it's quite easy.

As you can see, all these verbs are used with a non-finite. All these verbs are used here as auxiliaries. You can see, too, that *need* is behaving like a Peculiar – it is forming its negative by simply adding *not* (*n't*).

(2) *be, have, do* and *need*, as normal verbs:
   I *am* the teacher.
   That *is* my car.
   Be careful.
   The party *was* last night.
   I *have* a new book.
   We *had* a good meal today.
   The gardener *did* his work well.
   My exercise-book is full. I *need* a new one.

DARE USED TO

Two other Peculiars, *dare* and *used to*, always need a non-finite to complete them. They are always followed by the infinitive.

   Dare you **climb** (*infinitive without "to"*) that tree?
   I daren't **climb** it.
   *Used you **to climb** that tree when you were a boy?
   Yes, I used **to climb** it when I was a boy.
   *I usen't **to be** afraid then.

**Did you use to climb*? and *I didn't use to be afraid then* are more common now.

Notice these verbs act like Peculiars, a) they make their negative by using simply *not* (*n't*), b) they make their interrogative by inversion.

But *dare* can also make its interrogative and its negative as all the verbs except the Peculiars do, that is by using *do* and *do not*, e.g.

Did you *dare* to ask for another exercise-book?
I *didn't dare* ask for another exercise-book; my present one was not full.

So now that point is cleared up we can repeat our rule.

Auxiliary verbs help other verbs to form their tenses, moods, etc. They are not used alone but always with a non-finite.

Exercises

A What is a normal verb? In which of the following sentences are the verbs *be, do, need* and *have* used as auxiliaries; in which are they normal verbs?

  1 I did all my exercises correctly yesterday.
  2 Did Kofi get all his exercises correct?
  3 What time does the lesson start?
  4 Have you read this new book?
  5 I have a copy of it at home but I haven't read it yet.
  6 I want to move this table and I need your help.
  7 You needn't come at once if you are busy, we can do the job later.
  8 We have a big table. We need a big one for our family.
  9 What time is the football match? Is Zakari playing in it?
  10 We have been doing some painting, but we need some more paint. Have you any red paint that you are not using?

19 The Peculiars
The Emphatic Form

You have already been told a number of the peculiarities of the Peculiars, but there are quite a number of other things that you have not yet been told.

Sometimes when we are speaking, we want to be **emphatic**, that is, we want to put the matter rather more strongly. In speaking, we can do this by saying some particular word with more force. In writing we sometimes do this by underlining the word or printing it in italics, like this:

He thought I was not listening, but I <u>was</u> listening.
You think Mary is not clever, but she <u>is</u> clever.
Junaid says I can't climb that tree, but I *can* climb it.
I don't want to say this, but I *must* say it.
You believed the cat hadn't stolen the meat, but it *had*.
I don't want to punish the cat but I *will* punish it.
What can he mean by saying that? It *cannot* be true.

But the only verbs that we can emphasize like this are the Peculiars.

Suppose we want to emphasize a verb that is not one of the Peculiars. What do we do then?

Here is a little conversation that I expect you have heard several times before between Helen and me.

TEACHER Helen, you must try hard with your grammar.

HELEN (*feeling that I am being unfair*) But, sir, I do try hard with my grammar.

TEACHER You didn't try with that exercise I have just given you.

HELEN Sir, I did try hard with it.

TEACHER I don't think you took much care with it.

HELEN Oh yes, sir, I did take care with it.

TEACHER You don't spend much time on the work.

HELEN Oh, sir, I do spend a lot of time.

Did you notice how Helen emphasized the verbs *try, take, spend*?

When I said:

"You don't try." the unemphatic answer should be "I try."

"You didn't try," the unemphatic answer should be "I tried."

"You didn't take much care," the unemphatic answer should be "I took care."

"You don't spend," the unemphatic answer should be "I spend."

But she changed the answer

"I try" into "I *do* try."

"I spend" into "I *do* spend."

"I tried" into "I *did* try."

"I took" into "I *did* take."

The emphatic form of the verb is made by changing the finite verb into the infinitive and putting "do" (one of the Peculiars!) in front of it.

Here are some examples:

NON-EMPHATIC   EMPHATIC

Present Tense

I like chocolate.   I *do* like chocolate.
He hates being late for   He *does* hate being late
   school.   for school.
Yusuf works hard.   Yusuf *does* work hard.
Sit down.   *Do* sit down.

NON-EMPHATIC	EMPHATIC
Past Tense	
Mary cooked a good meal.	Mary *did* cook a good meal.
You sang that song well.	You *did* sing that song well.

Exercises

A Say the following sentences, stressing one of the verbs in each in order to make the sentences emphatic:
1 Phina can play the piano well.
2 Felix is a big boy for his age.
3 I shall be glad to be home again.
4 We were sorry you had to go so early.
5 You will try to come again, won't you?
6 I must get this work done before Friday.

B Write the following sentences in the Emphatic Form:
1 Victor likes cake.
2 He enjoyed the ones he ate at the party.
3 I like the food that Mrs Dina cooked.
4 We had a good swim this afternoon.
5 You bought a lot of chocolate.
6 Chiedu runs fast.
7 The wind blew hard when we were at sea.
8 You brought a lot of clothes with you.
9 Henry came here quickly.
10 Henry gets here quickly.
11 Akpan drank a lot of lemonade.
12 They took a long time to come here.
13 Those shoes I bought wore well.
14 He promised he would write and he wrote.
15 It rained hard last night.
16 You told me to see the picture at the cinema and I saw it.
17 He asked me to teach him French and I taught him.
18 You do these exercises well.

20 The Peculiars Question Phrases

You have noticed, I expect, those little "question phrases" that we often use in conversation. Instead of asking a question directly, we make a statement and put a question phrase at the end. This is what I mean:

Statement	Question Phrase
He is English,	isn't he?
You were there,	weren't you?
We shall go	shan't we?

The verb in the question phrase is always in the same tense as the verb in the statement.

In the first example above, the verb in the statement is present tense, *is*. The verb in the question phrase is present tense, *isn't*.

In the second example, the verb is in the past tense, *were*; so the verb in the question phrase is past tense, *weren't*.

In the third example, the verb is in the future tense, *shall*; so the verb in the question phrase is in future tense, *shan't*.

If the statement is affirmative the question phrase is negative.

Here are some examples:

Statement *Affirmative*	Question Phrase *Negative*
It's a nice day,	isn't it?
You can understand me,	can't you?
He will help us,	won't he?
They must answer,	mustn't they?
He was late	wasn't he?
I can play	can't I?

If the statement is negative, the question phrase is affirmative.

Here are some examples:

Statement Negative	Question Phrase Affirmative
I haven't explained this,	have I?
You don't understand this,	do you?
She wasn't asked,	was she?
She needn't come,	need she?
You haven't broken the cup,	have you?

If the verb in the statement is in the present tense (and is not one of the Peculiars) **we use "do" ("does"), "don't" ("doesn't") in the question phrase.**

Statement Affirmative	Question Phrase Negative
They know us,	don't they?
We know them,	don't we?
You understand that,	don't you?
He understands it,	doesn't he?
She speaks French,	doesn't she?

Statement Negative	Question Phrase Affirmative
They don't know us,	do they?
We don't know them,	do we?
You don't understand that,	do you?
He doesn't understand it,	does he?
She doesn't speak French,	does she?

If the verb in the statement is in the past tense (and is not one of the Peculiars) **we use "did" ("didn't") in the question phrase.**

Examples:

Statement Affirmative	Question Phrase Negative
They knew us,	didn't they?
You understood that,	didn't you?
She spoke French,	didn't she?

Statement	*Question Phrase*
Negative	*Affirmative*
They didn't know us,	did they?
You didn't understand that,	did you?
She didn't speak French,	did she?

You have heard phrases like those many times.
But have you noticed that:

The only verbs that can be used in "question phrases" are the Peculiars.

Exercises

A Add "question phrases" to the following. No. 1 is done for you.

1. You haven't finished yet, *have you*?
2. He didn't answer.
3. We can't come too.
4. I shan't see you tomorrow.
5. He mustn't speak.
6. I don't know him.
7. They oughtn't to speak.
8. He answered.
9. He daren't ask us.
10. He must speak.
11. We can come too.
12. I daren't ask her.
13. I shall see you tomorrow.
14. They ought to speak.
15. I know him.
16. He doesn't understand what we say.
17. They won't stay away tomorrow.
18. We can't take animals to school.
19. We mustn't spend all this money.
20. You couldn't answer all the questions.
21. It hasn't rained for weeks.
22. There isn't enough for all of us.
23. There won't be enough for all of us.
24. There will be enough for all of us.
25. We shan't have another lesson for a week.
26. Arit sings better than Mary.

27 Mary doesn't sing as well as Arit.
28 You've been here before.
29 You haven't been here before.
30 He never does what you tell him.
31 You didn't speak to him.
32 You spoke to him.
33 They sang a lot of songs.
34 They didn't sing many songs.
35 He writes to you often.
36 He wrote to you every day.
37 He didn't write to you every day.

21 Short Answers

Let's take another point about the Peculiars. Quite often when we are asked a question we give a "short answer", that is, we leave out part of the answer. An example will show what I mean. If you were asked the question "Do you go to school every day?" your answer could be, "Yes, I go to school every day," but you would be more likely to give the short answer: "Yes, I do." Here are some more examples of the full answer and the short answer.

Question	*Full answer*	*Short answer*
Have you brought your book?	Yes, I have brought my book.	Yes, I have.
Did you understand the lesson?	Yes, I understood the lesson.	Yes, I did.
Can you swim?	Yes, I can swim.	Yes, I can.
Doesn't Leo like grammar?	No, he doesn't like grammar.	No, he doesn't
Hasn't he finished the exercise?	No, he hasn't finished the exercise.	No, he hasn't.
Will the teacher be pleased?	No, he won't be pleased.	No, he won't.
Dare he climb that tree?	No, he daren't climb that tree.	No, he daren't.

And look at the verbs in the short answers!
Do you notice which they are?

There's another kind of short answer. Here are examples:
Question: Who is the stronger, Bingo or Jingo?
Long answer: Mr Jingo is the stronger.
Short answer: Mr Jingo is.

Question: Who can do this exercise?
Long answer: I can do this exercise.
Short answer: I can.

Question: Who must try harder?
Long answer: Hafiz must try harder.
Short answer: Hafiz must.

Question: Who will get into trouble if he doesn't try harder?
Long answer: Hafiz will get into trouble if he doesn't try harder.
Short answer: Hafiz will.

Question: Who dare climb that tree?
Long answer: Usman dare climb that tree.
Short answer: Usman dare.

With the present tense, for all verbs except the Peculiars we use "do", "does", "don't", "doesn't" for short answers.

Question: Who speaks English?
Long answer: I speak English.
Short answer: I do.

Question: Who often comes to school late?
Long answer: Chris often comes to school late.
Short answer: Chris does.

Question: Who doesn't understand this?
Long answer: I don't understand this.
Long answer: Sam doesn't understand this.
Short answer: I don't.
Short answer: Sam doesn't.

With the past tense, for all verbs except the Peculiars we use "did", "didn't".

Question: Who wrote this?
Long answer: I wrote it. OR John wrote it.
Short answer: I did. OR John did.

Question: Who didn't finish the exercise?
Long answer: I (or Ike) didn't finish the exercise.
Short answer: I (or Ike) didn't.

Notice again the verbs in those short answers!

Sometimes short answers are used to express agreement or disagreement, e.g.

Statement	Agreement
John is working hard.	Yes, he is.
Alhaji Zuru has a lot of money.	Yes, he has.
It was a wet day yesterday.	Yes, it was.
You've dropped your handkerchief.	So I have!
You said that before.	So I did.

Statement	Disagreement
Kwashie is working hard.	No, he isn't.
It will take a long time to do that.	No, it won't.
This book costs a lot of money.	No, it doesn't.
You said that before.	No, I didn't.
Why didn't you say you knew him?	But I did.
Dare Jibrin climb that tree?	No, he daren't.
You're late for your lesson.	Oh no, I'm not.

And once again the verbs in the short answers are our little friends *be, have, can, do,* etc.

The only verbs you can use in short answers are the Peculiars.

Exercises

A Give first the full answer and then the short answer (beginning "Yes") to the following questions:

1 Have you read this book?
2 Can you speak English?
3 Will you come for a walk?
4 Have you met my Uncle Adjei?
5 Are you boys playing football?
6 Must I be there at 4 o'clock?
7 Ought he to pay for these sweets?
8 Does Festus like cakes?
9 Were you at the party last night?
10 Is that boy with the brown shoes John?
11 Did you hear what he said?
12 Will you be fourteen tomorrow? (*Be careful with this one.*) (See Book, 3 p. 33)

LESSON 21

B Give first the full answer and then the short answer (beginning "No") to the following questions:
1. Have you spoken to him?
2. Can you swim across the river?
3. Have you been to London?
4. Are the girls playing in the field?
5. Ought he to be here today?
6. Does Joyce always give the right answers?
7. Did Joyce give the right answer yesterday?
8. Did the boys climb the tree?
9. Must I be there at four o'clock? (*There are four answers here.* See p. 59.)
10. Will you be fourteen tomorrow? (*Remember No. 12*)

C Give first the full answer, then the short answer, to each of the following questions:
1. Who is the better swimmer, Leila or Mary?
2. Who can open this door?
3. Who will help me to move this table?
4. Who did that exercise correctly?
5. Who didn't do the exercise correctly?
6. Who gets up every morning at seven o'clock?
   (*Give two answers,* (1) *beginning* "I...", (2) *beginning* "Kofi...")

D Agree with the following (use short answers):
1. It's raining hard now. Yes...
2. But it was worse yesterday. Yes...
3. That window is open. So...
4. Your Uncle Adjei gave you that bicycle. Yes...
5. I told you the answer yesterday. So...
6. There's a mouse eating that yam. So...

E Disagree with the following:
1. It is raining now? No ...
2. This train stops at Greenfields station. No...
3. It stopped there yesterday. No...
4. Why didn't you tell me so? But...
5. Ita likes to stay up late at night. Oh no,...
6. Alhaji Zuru has plenty of money. Oh no,...

22 The Peculiars Additions to Remarks

There is another fairly common construction in which we make an addition to a remark. Here's an example of what I mean.

Remark	Addition
Grace can play the piano,	and so can I.
We have a good teacher,	and so have you.
Etuk ought to work harder,	and so ought Sefi.
Our class will have a holiday tomorrow,	and so will yours.

Notice that when we make the addition we invert (Book 2, page 57) the verb and subject, e.g. *can I* (not *I can*); *have you* (not *you have*); *ought Sefi* (not *Sefi ought*).

With the present tense of all verbs except the Peculiars we use *do* (*does*).

John cycles to school every morning, *and so do I*.
I cycle to school every morning, *and so does John*.

With the past tense of all verbs except the Peculiars we use *did*.

Usman scored a goal, *and so did Leo*.
Mary came to school early, *and so did I*.
Mary worked hard, *and so did I*.

There is a negative form of this construction. In that case we use *neither* or *nor*, again with inversion of the subject and verb.

Here are some examples:

Mary can't play the piano, *neither (nor) can Agnes*.
We haven't a good teacher, *neither (nor) have you*.
Peter ought not to waste his time, *neither ought Bala*.
Our class won't have a holiday tomorrow, *neither will yours*.
Usman daren't climb that tree, *neither dare Rikku*.
Janet doesn't play the piano, *neither does Susan*.
John didn't score a goal, *neither did Ango*.
Leila mustn't do that, *neither must Grace*.

Notice that there is a negative in the remark, but an affirmative in the addition, i.e.
can (not *can't*), *have* (not *haven't*), *will* (not *won't*).
I don't think I need tell you which are the only verbs that can be used in additions!

Just one final point before we leave the Peculiars.
The usual position for such adverbs as *generally, never, always, sometimes, nearly, often*, is before the verb, e.g.
I *always* sleep with my windows open.
Michael *never* gets his exercise right.
We *often* cycle to school.
I *nearly* missed the train.
Mary *sometimes* cooks our meals.
But with some verbs they go after the verb. Can you guess which ones? Here are some examples:
I have *never* seen him.
He is *always* busy when I call.
Abbas can *always* find time for a game of football.
He is *often* late for school.
He may *sometimes* make a mistake; he doesn't *often* make one.
You needn't *always* do every exercise.
The usual place for the adverbs "generally, never, always, sometimes, nearly, often", etc., is after the Peculiars.

Exercises

A Add "additions" to these remarks. Don't forget the inversion. (The subject of the addition is given in brackets).
1 Gloria can't sing. (John)
2 Mary wasn't late for school. (Elizabeth)
3 Jumai hasn't a rich uncle. (Eno)
4 That cap isn't mine. (this)
5 Those books aren't mine. (these)
6 He oughtn't to say such things. (you)
7 We didn't know the right time. (they)
8 Mary doesn't stay up late at night. (Ada)
9 Joseph won't be fourteen tomorrow. (Ike)
10 Mary won't be fourteen tomorrow. (I) (*Be careful.*)

B Rewrite the following sentences putting the adverbs (in brackets) in the correct position.
1 I get up at seven o'clock (always).
2 He has done this before (never).
3 Ime and Chuka are early for school (generally). Samuel comes late (usually).
4 Mary comes to our house (often). Arit has come with her (often).
5 I think (sometimes) that Zakari will learn grammar (never).
6 We have finished our work (nearly); I forgot (nearly) it had to be done by six o'clock.
7 It is not easy (always) to do something that you have done before (never).
8 I have seen a fox in this area (never) but my father says he saw one (often) when he was a boy.
9 We go for a holiday (sometimes) in May and we have good weather (usually).
10 We go for a holiday in August (generally) and we have good weather (nearly always). (*Remember "had" is sometimes a full verb. Page 65.*)

23 A Word or Two on Punctuation

The aim of punctuation is to make the meaning of a passage more clearly and easily understood. A complete difference of meaning can be caused by a difference of punctuation. Look at these two sentences, for example. The words in each are exactly the same; it is the punctuation that makes the difference.

1 Simbi said, "The teacher is silly."
2 "Simbi," said the teacher, "is silly."

And there is an old story about a barber who put up a notice:

> What do you think
> I shave you for nothing
> And give you a drink

Customers came to his shop expecting a free shave and a free drink. But he explained that the notice should be read like this:

> What! Do you think I shave you for nothing and give you a drink?

Many of the most commonly used punctuation marks are illustrated in the examples given above; these are **quotation marks** or inverted commas (" "), used to show direct speech; the **exclamation mark** (!), used after an interjection or expression of strong feeling; the **question mark** (?), used after a direct question, but not after an indirect one; the **comma** (,) and the **full stop** (.).

The full stop, the colon (:), the semi-colon (;) and the comma are generally used to show the pause that you would make in speaking the words. The full stop marks the longest pause; the comma, the shortest pause; the semi-colon marks a longer pause than the comma but a shorter one than the colon.

The **full stop** is used:

1 at the end of all sentences except questions and exclamations, e.g.

> He needs your help. (*Statement*)
> Help him. (*Command*)
> Will you help him? (*Question*)
> He cried, "Help! Help!" (*Exclamation*)

2 after abbreviations such as M.A. (= Master of Arts), H.M.S. *Valiant* (= Her Majesty's Ship *Valiant*), U.S.A. (= United States of America), e.g. (= exempli gratia (*Latin*) = for example), etc.

The **colon** is used:

1 to separate sentences of which the second explains more fully the meaning of the first. It often means the same as "that is to say", e.g.

> Peter's work is unsatisfactory: his answers are thoughtless, his spelling is careless and his writing is bad.

2 to introduce a number of items in a list, e.g.

> Some commonly used punctuation marks are: full stop, colon, semi-colon and comma.

The **semi-colon** is useful when we need a longer pause than is indicated by a comma, but when we don't want to break the line of thought, as would happen if we used a full stop. It is used:

1 to separate co-ordinate sentences; especially when a conjunction is not used, e.g.

> "Your appearance pleased my friend; then it delighted me; I have watched your behaviour in strange circumstances; I have studied how you played and how you bore your losses; lastly, I have put you to the test of a staggering announcement, and you received it like an invitation to dinner." (R.L. Stevenson).

Note how, in this example, shorter pauses are shown by the commas.

2 with words like *so, therefore, however, nevertheless, besides, then, otherwise*. These words join sentences but are stronger than mere conjunctions like *and* or *but*, and so need a stronger punctuation mark. Here are some examples:

Do the work well; then I will pay you.
You must take more exercise; otherwise you will get too fat.
Adamu didn't work hard; so he didn't pass his examination.

The **comma** is the most frequently used punctuation mark and has many uses. Your common sense and the desire to make your meaning clear will often tell you where you want to make a pause, but these "rules", though they don't cover all the uses, may be helpful. A comma is generally used:

1 To record a list of objects, etc., e.g.:
At the party we had cakes, jellies, ices, biscuits, chocolate and lemonade.

Notice that the comma is not usually put before *and* and the last item.

2 To mark off direct speech:
"Tell me," he said, "how you know all that."
The friend replied, "I heard it on the radio."

3 To mark off sentences or clauses where a pause is needed in reading. This is almost always the case if the clause is an adverb one, e.g.:
Although it was wet, we played the match.
I have explained this work to Patrick, but he still doesn't understand it.
If you will help me, I will help you.
John, who is in our class, has won a scholarship.

4 To mark off words used in addressing a person, e.g.:
Bisi, tell Jimoh the answer to the question.
I hope, sir, my answer is right.

5 To mark off words or phrases like *however, therefore, of course, for instance*, etc.
You know, of course, what a gerund is: I needn't, therefore, explain it now.

6 In descriptive titles such as:
Elizabeth II, Queen of Great Britain...
I saw Mr Offor, your teacher, this morning.

7 To mark off phrases containing a participle when a pause is required in reading:

> Abdul, seeing that his brother was hurt, ran to help him.

> Remembering how fond you are of fruit, I've brought you some guava from our garden.

Exercise

Rewrite these stories, and put in the punctuation:

1 the following was written on the gravestone of an army mule here lies maggie the mule who in her time kicked a general two colonels four majors ten captains twenty-four lieutenants forty sergeants and two hundred and twenty privates she has finally kicked the bucket

2 its really wonderful said mr oruene what is wonderful asked his friend well said mr oruene look at these shoes im wearing the leather comes from new zealand it was tanned in yorkshire the shoes were stitched in wales the laces were woven in india the rubber soles came from malaysia and i bought them in a shoe shop in new york whats so remarkable about that asked his friend isnt it wonderful continued mr oruene taking no notice of the interruption that so many people in so many places should work to keep me from going barefoot

3 a very agitated woman rang up her doctor and a nurse answered the phone can i speak to dr omoigui she said its urgent im sorry madam the doctor is out will you leave a message oh dear oh dear my little boy has swallowed my watch when will the doctor be in im afraid madam hes gone to the teaching hospital and wont be back for two or three hours three hours cried the woman what shall i do in the meantime i suggest madam that you go to the casualty department of the nearest hospital without delay

Goodbye

Well, that's the end of *Brighter Grammar*. You've now had a general outline, a "bird's-eye view" of English Grammar and you've met some of the chief "rules". (They have been printed in heavy type so that you would remember them.) Just a word about those "rules" so that you don't get any wrong ideas. We don't want you to get a picture in your mind of an old grammarian, hundreds of years ago, saying to a very young English Language (just as a schoolmaster might speak to a rather disobedient little boy):

"So you are the English Language, are you? Well, my boy, here's a list of rules that I have made, and you have got to obey them!"

That's quite a wrong picture. The English Language came long before the grammarian. Grammarians are merely people who have observed the language at work and have said, "So far as we can see, this is how the English Language works. We've studied it at work and we've written down what we have observed. Sometimes it behaves like other languages, like French or German for example. Sometimes (you remember the Peculiars) it behaves quite differently from other languages." Their attitude is like Newton discovering the law of gravity or modern scientists exploring the atom. These scientists don't say, "Look, Nature, here are some laws that you must obey." Scientists don't work like that. They say rather, "We have studied Nature and tried to discover its working, and this is what we have discovered. These, so far as we can see at present, are the laws of Nature."

In *Brighter Grammar* we have tried to approach grammar in the same "scientific" way. In these books you have seen us and John, Arit and Mary (and even Rufai!) trying to see how the language works and to tell you what we discover. We have tried to show you that English Grammar is not a collection of dull, dead words but a living thing. It is a living tree, slowly but constantly growing and changing; not a dead, decaying log. Some of its limbs may gradually die and fall away (the subjunctive is one of them), but new life springs out at the tips of its branches; new words, new constructions take the place of those that die.

And when you see grammar in this light, then we believe that "dreary grammar" becomes "brighter grammar".

Phebean Ogundipe
C.E. Eckersley
Margaret Macaulay